BOOKED IT!

Selling, Closing and Standing Out in the

Special Events Industry

MERYL SNOW

Printed in the United States of America

First Printing, 2016

ISBN: 1548048658
ISBN - 13: 978-1548048655

Dedication

To **MY** Andy- I still can't believe you're not sick of me!
You are my world.

To **MY** Kelly- we stopped at perfection.
Always my bestie.

In memory of Michael Roman- mentor and friend-
I tip my hat.

Table of Contents

INTRODUCTION

Weddings, galas and birthday bashes. Album release parties, charity fundraisers, and product launches. Corporate retreats, meetings, exhibitions and conferences. What do all special events have in common? They can't plan themselves. As such, each of these events needs to have a focused and committed team working together to accomplish the goal of a perfectly planned event for the client. Individuals often find out that they lack the much-needed expertise and time to plan events themselves. This is where we as independent event professionals step in and give these special events the special attention they so much deserve. The special events industry is one that has grown tremendously in the past decade with around $500 billion spent annually for special events worldwide. The events industry is multifaceted. This means that the marketplace that the event industry provides is big enough to support your endeavor as an event professional. There are many directions in which you can expand and the industry provides a lucrative market ready to sustain you. From wedding planners to caterers to venue coordinators, floral designers and entertainers, the tasks are myriad.

Before the Internet, the event professionals were the experts, coming up with the answers and ideas. Today, roles have been reversed with the clients doing researches. Let's take the modern wedding as an example; today's couple has a wide array of information sources from bridal magazines, the Internet, wedding books, wedding TV shows. They simply have many things to look to, with bridal magazines constantly churning out issues like 'Secrets for big day savings', 'Questions to ask before you book'. There is seemingly an information overload and the clients come asking questions because what they're reading is telling them to ask the questions. She is armed and ready. Are you? The difficulty of 'selling' in the special events market is compounded by the fact that today's clients have a wide array of options available to them as regards what they can buy. Hence, there is a need to understand the client, set yourself apart from the competition, and show your client how you're different in order to close sales. It is only necessary to stand out from other event professionals like you. Just how do you do this? Sell yourself. The phrase "sell yourself" is most often misinterpreted as showcasing your positive features and throwing yourself in the face of people whom you intend to make an impression on, however selling yourself is more about pulling clients to your company.

Perhaps your bookings have started to drop off lately, and you find yourself struggling to hit sales targets that you used to breeze right past. You may be fabulous at bonding with the client but still find yourself losing opportunities. It is not just enough to bond with the client. Have you ever met with a client and you instantly connected? You just have the confidence that you will book the event. A week later, the client is not responding to your calls and emails. What happened? You were outsold! No matter how hard you work, how well you qualify and regardless of how well you think your meeting with the client went, if you are weak at closing sales, you will suffer in your career in the events industry. Closing sales involves a calculated process of understanding the client's needs, showing the client that you have what it takes to fill that need and ultimately, creating a relationship with the client so that he decides to trust you with the job of filling that need they have. How do you go about this, you ask? How do you reignite your passion in sales and go from no clients to fully booked? What sales techniques are to be employed to propel your events company to higher heights?

These and many more questions are answered in this book. It is a guide to get you started as a highly effective, amazingly memorable event professional; think of it as a behind-the-scenes road map for kick-starting sales and getting fresh perspective, ideas and motivation for your special events company.

Chances are you are in the event industry because you have a passion for what you do. We are in an industry that asks us to sell, plan and execute the event and that is three completely different skill sets.

CHAPTER 1

WHO ARE YOU?

A great sales tool that many of us tend to overlook is our personality. Personality plays an important role in sales and in the workplace. Anyone might be able to sell if the price is cheap enough or if what is being sold is something that people cannot live without, like air. The truth, however, is that neither of these luxuries are part of the scenario for a vast majority of us. You might say 'But I am not exactly a salesperson, I am an event professional'. Keep in mind that you are selling yourself first. If you think you're not a salesperson - think again. In some way, all humans are in sales. You sell yourself every day. A mother tries to get her child into a prestigious private school, in some way, this is sales. You go on a first date dressed to the nines; you are in some way selling yourself. In the events business as well, who are you does matter. A little bit of introspection is required, what are my core strengths as a person? Where do I need to improve? Knowing this is vital to your success at sales.

The dynamics of performance depends to a great extent on an individual's personality. To this end, many organizations use personality profiling to build their teams. I had an employee that I thought totally disrespected me. I would send him an email and I knew he opened it because of the read receipt. However, he didn't answer me right away.

My personality- I read the email, type my response and send it immediately. His personality- He reads the email, thinks about it. Then in a day, reads it again and thinks more about it and then sleeps on it and then later in the week replies to the email. Neither of us is right or wrong, two people have different approaches. What is important is that we know each other's traits. Now when I send him an email, I don't expect it right away and when he receives an email, he knows that I would like a response soon. The personalities of individuals you bring onboard have a tremendous effect on the efficiency of your company. This is so because a company's efficiencies or inefficiencies are brought about by performances and behavior of employees in the first place and this primarily depends on their personalities.

Personality tests – questionnaires or other standardized instrument designed to reveal areas of an individual's character or psychological makeup – tend to get people thinking about the role of personality in the workplace. More companies rely on the personality test to measure an applicant's job value.

It helps you understand where your team members' strengths and weaknesses lie. There are several tests such as the DISC, The Caliper Profile, Gallup StrengthsFinder, and Myers-Briggs Type Indicator.

Personality tests were developed for the workplace in the 1940s and 1950s by research teams at industrial companies like AT&T Inc. These tests were first used basically to screen candidates for management jobs. Employers wanted to know, for instance, if a potential executive was an extrovert, prone to anxiety or an office backstabber. The tests fell out of favor in the 1960s, after researchers questioned their reliability, only to resurface in the 1990s, when industrial psychologists determined they had value as a hiring tool.

For the past decade, about 80% of Fortune 500 companies have utilized a psychometric test. One being Myers-Briggs Type Indicator to study the personalities of new hires. The Myers–Briggs Type Indicator (MBTI) is an introspective questionnaire that is designed to indicate psychological preferences in how individuals perceive the world and make their decisions. The personality test uses a series of yes or no questions to break down personalities along four dichotomies: Introversion (I) versus Extraversion (E); Thinking (T) versus Feeling (F);

Sensing (S) versus Intuitive (N) and Perceiving (P) versus Judging (J). These generate four-letter combinations that represent an individual's psychological type. There are 16 possible types, with all being equal and none the best. Each person fits into one of the 16 types.

ISTJ The Duty Fulfillers	**ISFJ** The Nurturers	**INFJ** The Protectors	**INTJ** The Scientists
ISTP The Mechanics	**ISFP** The Artists	**INFP** The Idealists	**INTP** The Thinkers
ESTP The Doers	**ESFP** The Performers	**ENFP** The Inspirers	**ENTP** The Visionaries
ESTJ The Guardians	**ESFJ** The Caregivers	**ENFJ** The Givers	**ENTJ** The Executives

PERSONALITY TYPES The goal of knowing about personality type is to understand and appreciate differences between people. As all types are equal, there is no best type.
SOURCE: MYERSBRIGGS.ORG

There are certain, innate personality traits and professional attitudes that are essential to becoming a great event professional. The special events industry is one that is majorly about people and your relationships with them. It's all about the client and working together with other people to reach the common goal of a great event. Today, the average client has a wide range of options available to them in regards to whom they entrust their event. In order to close the sale, it becomes necessary for you – your company to stand out from other event professionals. Personality greatly influences sales in the events business. Selling comes easily to the ESTP, ENFJ, ESFP and ENFP personalities.

- ESTP – These are flexible and tolerant individuals who they take a pragmatic approach focused on immediate results. Theories and conceptual explanations bore them; they would rather act energetically to solve the problem. They put their focus on the here-and-now. They are spontaneous and enjoy each moment that they can be active with others. They learn best through doing.

- ENFJ – These are warm, responsive, empathetic, and responsible individuals. They are highly attuned to the emotions, needs, and motivations of other people. They are loyal, responsive to praise and criticism. Sociable, facilitate others in a group, and provide inspiring leadership. They find potential in everyone and as such want to help others fulfill their potential. ENFJs may act as catalysts for individual and group growth.

- ESFP – Naturally outgoing, friendly and accepting people. They love life and people and enjoy working with others to make things happen. They make work fun and bring common sense and a realistic approach to their work. Flexibility and spontaneity are some of their traits as they adapt readily to new people and environments. They learn best by trying new skills with other people.

- ENFP – They are warmly enthusiastic and imaginative individuals who see life as full of possibilities. They can make connections between events and information very quickly and then proceed confidently based on the patterns they see. They readily give their appreciation and support. They are usually spontaneous, flexible and often rely on their ability to improvise and their verbal fluency.

Did you notice that these personalities all have one thing in common? They are extraverts. There are hardly any sales positions where a salesperson can get away with never having to speak to a customer. The events industry is similar because it revolves a lot around meeting clients. People who tend toward extraversion are able to connect better with prospects every day. Extraverts' energy is directed primarily outward, towards people and things outside of themselves. They tend to be more demonstrative, speak and gesture better than introverts. The enthusiasm they show is likely to make prospects and clients have trust and confidence in them. Many extraverts find it easier to make small talk. In the events industry, being able to establish human rapport and relating to clients outside of the business is beneficial. Introverts, on the other hand, direct their energy inward, towards their own thoughts, perceptions, and reactions. Therefore, extraverts tend to be more naturally active, expressive, social, and interested in many things, whereas introverts tend to be more reserved, private, cautious, and interested in fewer interactions, but with greater depth and focus.

This is not to say that only those four personality types can succeed in the events business. However, the nature of an individual's personality has specific impacts on people who come across with and interact with that person. Often times, there is a great need for intensive level of communication with various stakeholders – the clients, your in-house employees, other events professionals, and suppliers in order to ensure the success of a special event. Managers of event companies who have extraverted personalities and excellent communication

skills would be in good position to establish communications with the many stakeholders and thus achieve high organizational efficiency. Although selling doesn't come naturally to introverts, they as well can learn and excel at selling. This requires adequate preparation. In the event business, it is vital that you put your best foot forward. You may not be the social, extraverted type but this does not imply that the events industry is not for you. Certain areas in your business might definitely not be your forte. If you find yourself dreading meetings with clients, then that task is due for delegating. If it fills you with anxiety or fear every time you have to do it, it might be time to select another person whose strengths lie in this. This is where surrounding yourself with the right people comes in. Having the right individuals with you, as part of your team is not only vital, it is a must. It is important that you have quality employees that can help your company run and grow. Surround yourself with teammates that have strengths in areas where you need to make improvements. This is a strong need to have a well-rounded team. Many people make the mistake of hiring after their personality. Many pick people who are like them. This limits diversity. Diversity is an indispensable part of any well-rounded workplace. Every company can benefit from a good mix of people.

CHAPTER 2

YOU AS A BRAND

One of the greatest ways to articulate your competencies, wealth of experience, skills, knowledge, and your overall worth in today's competitive events industry is to create and nurture a brand that helps you stand out in the crowd.

I was speaking at a national business conference in May, and I asked all of the salespeople in the audience to raise their hand. There were 300 attendees, and maybe 25 people raised their hands. Then I asked, "Have you ever tried to persuade a child to eat their vegetables? Have you ever tried to convince someone that your way is better, easier, or faster? Raise your hand if you have ever tried to convince, persuade, or influence someone." All hands rose. Everyone is selling something. From the moment you engage with someone they are judging you. First they judge what you wear and how you speak, then they judge what you're selling, and finally they judge your company. When you think of Donald Trump, (before his presidential campaign) what comes to mind: his hair, his ego, his fortune, or maybe his famous line, "You're fired"? That is his brand. Businesses have a brand, celebrities have a brand, and even you have a brand. Everyone has a brand. Your brand is your unique set of skills, talents, and know-how.

the moment you
ENGAGE
with someone, they are
judging
you
first, then they are
judging
what they are
BUYING

As aptly put by a management expert Tom Peters, "We are CEOs of our own companies: Me Inc. To be in business today, our most important job is to be head marketer of a brand called You."

Branding is a means of defining you, your business or company to yourself, your team and people on the outside – the potential clients. Creating an inimitable and powerful brand starts with determining what makes you unique. What are your strengths, goals, passions, and core competencies? What makes you different from your peers? It is not just enough to know what makes you unique, if you do not target the right people, the efforts are futile. There is a strong need to identify your target audience. This allows you to deliver and 'register' your company on the minds of the right people. Everything you do contributes to your branding endeavor, either positively or negatively. Even the little things count – dressing, behavior to employees, body language, emails, down to behavior on social media. If you want to be successful, creating and managing a brand isn't just an option, it's a necessity.

ENHANCING YOUR BRAND

While everyone has a brand, the only way for people to know your brand is for you to market it. Marketing and relationship building are one and the same, which is why I believe that marketing oneself is a life skill everyone must learn.

In order to sell yourself, you need to know yourself. Make a list of words that best describe your personality. What ideas and thoughts pop up as soon as someone hears your name? Are you creative, organized, dependable, fun, or motivational? Try not to list what you do for a career; instead list how you do it to be successful. Don't be modest.

For example, if you are a florist, you don't just make flower arrangements. What is your process to get the final arrangement? Is there a particular color palette that inspires you? Are you passionate about interior or geometric design? Do you have a keen ability to read clients and interpret the feeling they want to express through the arrangements you provide for them?

Try this exercise by filling in the blanks:

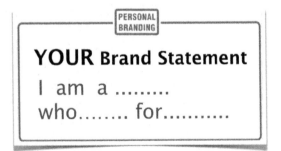

14

I am a _____ who _____ for _____

Here is an example:

I am a thriving event professional (with a passion for fashion) who has engaged solid planning and style for hundreds of successful events, during which I have remained calm and composed.

When you're selling you, it's important to show your personality: your likes, dislikes, life story, insecurities, and fears. Your ability to market your talents, achievements, and values inside your organization and within your profession, industry, and community are key parts of enhancing your brand.

The most efficient way to promote you is to allow the conversation to become give-and-take. Through natural dialogue, the client will realize that you are intelligent, capable, and have or can acquire the desired skills. After you return from a networking event or a meeting with a client, ask yourself: how engaging, relatable, confident, friendly, and trustworthy was I? Learn from every meeting, and continue to improve on how you are portraying your brand and marketing yourself.

At times our industry is merely seen as a commodity. Chicken is chicken; a flower is a flower. The client needs to be educated, but in order to be open to learning they need to like, trust, and

believe in you. The event industry can be saturated, at times, with excellent products. A good product keeps you in the game, but it certainly doesn't set you apart. How can you stand out from the competition? When all things are equal, people buy from people they like. Be sure to spend more time selling yourself instead of merely focusing on your product. Make friends, build trust, and the rest will come.

CHAPTER 3

COMPANY BRAND

Every business has a brand whether you know it or not. Branding is not only for the big companies. It's not just your logo, your tagline or slogan. They are signatures of your brand. Popular belief is that branding is a communication strategy. It is not. Branding is a business strategy, a way to align every action to guide your business to success. It is a phenomenon that happens in the mind and in the heart, it's a feeling one gets when they think of a product or company. The easiest way to describe branding is to think about it as a personality. It's an attitude. How it walks, how it talks, it tells a story about the company. Branding affects people on an emotional level. They need to know, like and trust your business.

In order to brand your company effectively, you must know who you are. First you will need to lay the foundation and ask yourself these questions:

- What is my core motivation?
- Who are my target clients?
- How does my company affect people on an emotional level?
- What problems am I solving for my market?
- What sets me apart from my competition?

List out your business's key features and characteristics, your competitive advantages. You need to know what it is that makes you different, special and more compelling than other event professionals in the market. Many companies, for example, spend much of their time, money and energy promoting their products and services instead of building their brand image. If you have a bakery shop and your main emphasis is on your cakes, then you don't have a brand, you have a commodity. There is the need to clearly define your unique marketing position. You need to show value and a clear understanding of why you are different from that other event professional down the street.

After completing the above exercises, then write a one-page mission statement, a company overview. This is not only intended to let your target market know who you are, but also the ideas, principles and values that you and your entire company will live by. Branding is not solely what you say; it's how you act. Remember it is a personality.

Let's take a closer look inside your business. In the hospitality industry your employees are in front, they are at times the company's voice.

- How does your staff look while they are setting up events? Are they disheveled, or are they in logo set up shirts?
- Do they use proper grammar?
- How do they dress?
- Are they following up with the clients?
- Are they knowledgeable of the company's services and goals?
- Do they represent your brand?

You must take control of your brand. If you don't manage your brand the market will do it for you. In order to establish brand awareness, branding needs to be used consistently and frequently in everything your produce.

Some years ago, it was very easy to manage your brand. You can control your message with print media, website and email marketing. Most companies would concentrate their efforts on their word-of-mouth reputation. Confident that if they did a good job for clients, the clients would tell their friends; fearful if they didn't, the client would also tell their friends. Whichever the case, friend or foe, word of mouth was a slow process indeed. Of course, word of mouth is still a powerful tool. What people say about you does have an effect on your brand. However, today the game has changed. Word of mouth has gone viral- within seconds your company may be mentioned in blogs, chat rooms, Facebook, Tweets, review channels and a myriad of other social media outlets. As such, you can and must manage your brand. How then do you manage your brand? Brand awareness takes time and effort. As a first step, it is pertinent that you find out what is already out there about you in the universe.

- Google your name and your company name. It is imperative that you know what's available on the Internet. Remember, potential clients will Google you and your company.

- Sign up to socialmention.com. It is free and this site will alert you via email when your name or company is mentioned in any social media arenas. This site will list percentages on how the mentions were used. Valuable information.

- Google Alert is a free service as well and it gives you email updates when your name or company name is mentioned on the web.

- Search.Twitter.com tells you what has been tweeted about you.

Branding is a business strategy for success. If you are satisfied with what is being said about you and your company, kudos! You've done a good job. However, you can't stop now; you must monitor your brand and continue with buzz-worthy content. This is done by your actions and managing your accounts.

LEVERAGING SOCIAL MEDIA

Social media is a viable tool for marketing your products and services and managing your brand identity. It is inexpensive, easy to work with and offers a great network of potential clients. Daily, millions of people use social networking applications. Social media is all about conversation and building effective relationships. Facebook, Twitter, Google+, Instagram amongst others are all avenues to sell yourself. Social media is powering the world in ways we could never have imagined years back. Today, connections are formed out of thin air. Imagine the millions of people that daily use social networking applications. Did you know that 22% of Americans use social media multiple times in a single day? Selling yourself in today's competitive market involves a savvy use of social media. There are tons of social media applications and websites available; however there is need to choose carefully before investing your time and energy in one. You should invest in a platform that supports your brand image.

To date, Facebook remains the best platform for creating brand awareness – its user base is diverse and nearly 75% of adult Americans use it. Tell me, how then is this not a wonderful channel through which you could build your brand and sell yourself to the world? Setting up a Facebook page isn't enough. It needs to be interactive, drive conversation and promote your brand all at the same time. If you only promote your products and services you will lose viewers. Try adding interesting tidbits, for example, a blurb about the history of pasta. To encourage conversation, you could post trivia and questions like "when you were growing up, what was your favorite comfort food?" Endeavor to provide your followers with something that piques their interest and that they can as well share to other people. With Facebook, there is the option of Facebook group page or business (fan) pages. Business and fan pages let you measure your traffic.

With fan pages, you can add feeds from other applications like YouTube Box, Flicker, and Twitter. For Facebook groups, you don't have that many options. When your fans take action on your page, their actions will be documented on the news feeds of their personal pages. Their friends could see the news feeds and check out your business page. Fan pages stand out on profiles, whereas group pages get lost in the mix. Fan pages enable you to provide unlimited news or updates to your fans while Facebook groups are limited to a definite number.

Businesses, especially those that rely heavily on images have lately have been flocking to Instagram in droves and rightly so because Instagram allows you to sell yourself by posting images and short videos relevant to your brand. Are you in the catering line? How about posting savory, colorful photos of wholesome food? Pinterest is also a wonderful social network where you can reach people. Video sharing services like YouTube allow you to add captivating videos of your products and services. When using YouTube, make sure you properly brand the beginning and end of your video with contact information. Blogging is also a wonderful way to sell your brand. Start a blog that is attached to your Facebook and website. Search engines easily pick up blogs. Platforms such as WordPress and Joomla make it easy to promote yourself to your target audience. On these platforms, you could post on topics that would pique the interest of your audience and they would find educational while at the same time highlighting your unique skills and experience. Did you know that Blog posts with images receive 94% more views? Don't be afraid to make use of visual content. Email marketing is also very beneficial. You could send an email blast teaser to direct people to your Facebook, blog or website. Another way could be adding link icons of your blogs, Facebook pages and Twitter accounts to your email signature and all Internet direct mail. Keep in mind that people who post on your Facebook page, Tweet about you or comment on your blog want to be heard. It is extremely important that you engage with your social community and answer or comment promptly.

With building your brand on social media, you should be careful who is representing your brand. Your employees play a big part in brand management and will need to be screened by you. This is important with all social network sites. Every single piece of content shared should support your brand identity. Poor choices of content or images tend to reflect poorly on your company. Set guidelines for your team to follow, suggest different accounts for business and personal and encourage them to play an active role in the company brand strategy.

The old expression, it's not what you know; it's who you know holds true in this new age marketing strategy. Continue to tweet, blog and post and watch your efforts flourish.

CHAPTER 4

SET YOURSELF APART

How can you set yourself apart from the competition? Think differently. In everything that you do, you have to be different from your competitors and show your client how you are different. It can be difficult to stand out. I have had the opportunity to survey hundreds of event professionals. On asking them to rank themselves on certain skills – bonding with the clients, planning and logistics, closing the sales and qualifying the client, the results were quite surprising. 41% ranked themselves highest on bonding with the client, 34% on planning and logistics, but only 13% was closing the sales and 12% was qualifying the client. Yikes, qualifying and closing is what we do.

Survey
Rank Yourself on these Skills

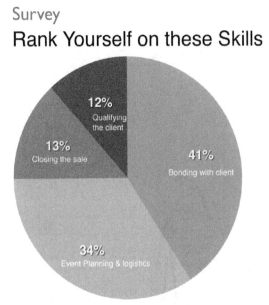

474 event sales professionals

It's just not enough to bond with the client. With the sharp difference between the number of those bonding with the client and those actually closing the sales, your entire business relies on qualifying the client and closing the sale! These two aspects are the most important. No matter how hard you work and regardless of how well you think your meeting and bonding with the client went, if you are weak in closing sales, you will suffer in your career. Learning certain sales skills can take sales performance to a whole new level.

There are six critical skills needed to create dialogue, understand the clients' needs, priorities and perspective and indeed close profitable business. These are:

- Presence – Ability to project confidence, conviction, and interest in body language and voice

- Relating – Ability to use acknowledgement, rapport and empathy to connect

- Questioning – Ability to explore needs and create dialogue

- Positioning – Ability to leverage client needs to be persuasive

- Listening – Ability to understand content and emotional message

- Checking – Ability to elicit feedback

Exercise

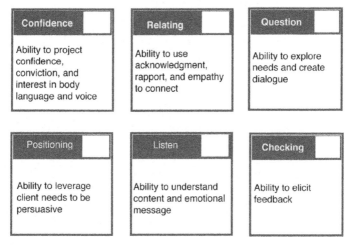

Confidence	Relating	Question
Ability to project confidence, conviction, and interest in body language and voice	Ability to use acknowledgment, rapport, and empathy to connect	Ability to explore needs and create dialogue

Positioning	Listen	Checking
Ability to leverage client needs to be persuasive	Ability to understand content and emotional message	Ability to elicit feedback

Rank yourself on these skills (1 to 6) with 1 being your greatest strength.

I would want you to rank yourself on each of these skills using numbers 1 – 6, with 1 being your greatest strength. All of the above skills are vital and should ideally be in your 1, 2 and 3s. Having skills in the range of 1,2,3 means you are good at them. Nonetheless, if you have any skills as 4, 5, or 6; it simply means you have to work on them. If you are able to master all 6 skills, you become a better salesperson. Having done the exercise, take a picture of it, print it out and put it by your computer. When you have to meet with a client, look at those skills you have as 4, 5 or 6, and say to yourself; "Today I have a meeting, and I'll work on this particular skill" Plan how you intend to do it.

CHAPTER 5

VITAL STAGES OF A SALE

There are six stages in sales. There is the necessity to **ask and listen**, **educate** the client, **know the client's needs**, present the **solution**, gain their **trust** and then **close** the sale.

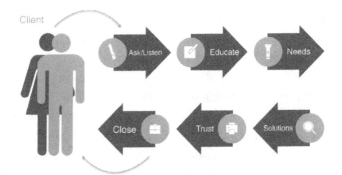

Vital **Stages** of a Sale

- **Ask and listen.** Questioning is a vital skill in communication. Asking the right questions allows you gain an insight into the mind of the client. Questions are utilized to explore the feelings, ideas, opinions and attitudes of your client; to clarify something they have said; to obtain information. When the right questions are asked, you are able to learn more about the client, understand them better and your decision-making process is aided. Anybody can

29

ask questions, however, to be successful at sales, there is a need to know how to ask questions. Two major types of questions are the close-ended and the open-ended. With clients, is it the open or the close? A close-ended question is one that can be answered with either a 'Yes' or 'No'. It is very easy for a client to just say 'Yes' or 'No' but you would not find out much when they do that. Open-ended questions, on the other hand, are those that receive a long answer, other than just a yes or no. Open-ended questions enable your client to think and reflect, they let you in on the client's opinions and feelings. Rather than simply ask yes or no questions, how about you ask questions that really elicit deeper responses like *'What do you think about that?'* *'To what extent is that happening?'* *'I'd love to hear your views on the issue, what are your perspectives?'* It is not about asking if they want the blue or pink linen. It is about asking really drawn out questions. Open-ended questions usually begin with words like what, why, describe and your objective is to get the client to talk as much as possible. When you ask questions, AND LISTEN, you really get to know your client and you would be surprised how well they are able describe their entire event for you. Probing a client with open-ended questions lets you get to the point quicker. In communicating with the client, there is need to listen as well, actively. Remain silent after you ask a question; give the client time to think it over. Suppose I ask a room full of people the question; *'What is in my bag?'* Respondents could ask close-ended questions like *'Is it lipstick?'* *'Is it a book'*, etc. and I could simply answer *either 'Yes'* nor *'No'* all day. With this, we could go on and on, spending time, a long time before getting to the answer. But being asked an open-ended question like *'Describe what is in your bag'* gets to the point way quicker because it draws out response.

- **Educate the client.** While it may be safe to assume today's clients are better informed, it's not safe to assume they are fully informed. Part of a successful selling strategy still includes client education. Who better to guide them towards smart decisions than you – the expert?

- **Know the client's needs**. This is where researching a potential client comes into play. You'll need to do your homework with an investigative nose. It is vital that you find out the type of person or organization you're meeting with and approach accordingly. For instance, while some prospects would hold you in high esteem when you show up in a complete business suit, some others would appreciate you in a more casual outfit. It's all about researching and finding out about the client's personality and needs beforehand in order to make a good impression.

- **Present a solution.** Now that you have researched on the client and found out about their needs, you should prepare your event ideas and plans to show to the client, tailored to their needs. Always bear in mind that the event is about the client, not you. Therefore, you should listen to the client's input and pay attention to what they have to say. Don't be quick to dismiss the client's ideas because they don't meet your standard. Again, it's their event and your job is to contribute to making it an amazing one based on the client's needs. But, don't be a yes person, it's your expertise that they are relying on, you'll need to guide them if something may not work. Be client-centric. Focus on making the client happy by helping them have the event of their dreams. Your goal is to listen to their vision and make it reality. The ideas and solutions you pitch to a client should reflect the values that the client seems to advocate. For some clients, what is important to them is to have the event of the decade, a talk-of-the-town event that sets the standard. For some other clients, all they may want is an event that makes their family members and friends happy. Pay attention, because if you don't, you'll never know what the client really wants.

- **Gain the client's trust**. People like to work with people they trust. You gain a client's trust by showing genuine interest in them and building rapport. If possible, arrange meetings in relaxed environments. A client needs to trust you to fill their needs. Be friendly to the client. No, I'm not talking about punching the client playfully or stroking their hair. I'm talking about creating rapport, understanding them, remembering your research and becoming a reflection of what they desire. Remember, besides the client booking you for their event, it is even easier for a friend to refer you to another client.

- **Close the sale.** This is a crucial aspect of sales. It's not just enough to build rapport and bond with the client. You should be closing deals! This aspect of sales is examined in a later chapter.

CHAPTER 6

Qualifying and
UNDERSTANDING THE BRIDE

Meet Sarah. Sarah is 28 years old, pretty girl, graduated from Harvard Law School, with honors. She works for a prestigious firm in Philadelphia. Suddenly, she begins to feel funny and goes to the doctor, saying: 'I just don't feel like myself. Everything feels off'. The doctor runs tests and everything comes back normal. She leaves the doctors office, only to return a couple of weeks later, still not feeling like herself. The doctor is perplexed. He asks; 'Has anything changed in the last couple of months?' To this, she says "No! everything couldn't be better. I have a great job and wonderful family and friends. Sarah paused a moment and then casually mentions that she recently was engaged. The doctor says "Oh! You know what you are, you're a bride!" We all know when brides get engaged, they totally change.

Are you one of the many who shy away from weddings purely because you just don't know what the bride really wants?

Or simply because you think it's too much handholding? I'm hoping to sway you. Years ago, brides' only sources of information were bridal magazines, dress shops and word of mouth. We as the event professionals were the go-to people, the experts who could educate the bride. This was indeed extremely time-consuming. Today, the biggest game changer has been the Internet; making it so simple that it's ridiculously easy for a bride not only to educate herself but to know exactly how her wedding will unfold. Ahhh, weddings! You best be ready for you can't fool today's bride. She has done her homework long before she meets with you. Today's bride knows the trends even before you do. She is scouring the vast amount of data on the internet, creating a wedding website of their 'must haves', reading every wedding book she can get her hands on and watching all the popular wedding TV shows. She has a Pintrest Board and subscribes to at least 50 wedding blogs. She is armed and ready. But are you?

Wonderful as the Internet education seems, the bride still needs your guidance; however, they look at you as a commodity. She thinks: chicken is chicken, a table is a table, a room is a room. Now more than ever is when you need to show your differences from your competitors. One would think that I am strictly talking about the differences of the company. No, I am not. The first sale that is made is YOU. The moment you engage with a bride, she is judging you first, then she's judging what she's buying and then she's judging the company.

Selling weddings require an entirely different mindset than corporate or other social events. From the initial phone call, this bride will be attached to you for months. She wants instant responses to phone calls and emails or she will tend to feel that her wedding isn't important to you. The selling process needs to be an experience for the couple, one that reinforces their belief that they are "special". They may want to meet in the evening or on a Saturday when you have six events. You must gladly be accommodating and adapt to their schedules or they will go down the list and meet with your competitor.

Before the initial phone call, you should go to her Pinterest page. There it is! Her entire wedding laid out right before your eyes in full color. You now know she loves peonies and pastels, prefers casual elegance versus formal sophistication and her three favorite specialty cocktails. This kind of information is priceless when building a relationship with the bride. Armed with such information, you can show her that you are different from the others. She likes you and thinks that you "get her."

Ask open-ended questions but make sure you really listen to the answers. Too often we ask a question and while they are answering, we are busy forming the next question in our minds. You can learn a great deal simply by listening. An excellent starter question is *"how did he propose?"* She will be taken off guard because she has never been asked this by previous industry pros and is used to being asked routine questions. Believe me; a bride will always talk about how she got engaged. By doing this, you have broken the barrier of a sales person into friend territory. Now it will be easy for a back and forth conversation which will lead to knowing so much about the event without asking the *'who, what, where, when'* that is the norm. Ask the couple how they envision their wedding day or ask them what do you want your guests to think when they leave your wedding and the floodgates open. Let's assume you are a photographer and you ask, what comes to mind when you think of a professional photographer? She may say, I don't even want a photographer, my mother is insisting. I can't stand posed photos, flash bulbs in my eyes and completely missing my cocktail party. Now you know exactly what she doesn't want which makes it so much easier to write the proposal. When she receives the proposal, she will be thrilled and say- wow, he gets me. Listen to every word. They want to be heard. As an event pro, your role is to paint a picture, tell a story. Their story. It's their big day. And it is filled with emotion; from the moment the first guests arrive until the bride and groom are swept away to their honeymoon.

Not every fiancé is as interested in wedding planning as their eager bride wants them to be (although some really are!) – but no matter what, it is key that you keep him engaged by asking questions about what he would like to see at the wedding and what is important to him. The bride will most likely have a large file or sometimes a suitcase of clippings from magazines. Be prepared. Have your checklist ready.

The bond of an event professional and bride has evolved. You will discuss not only the demi-glace on the filet or the linen color or the type of flowers for décor; but also her future sister-in-law who is driving her crazy because she doesn't like how the bridesmaid dress looks on her. If you're thinking that you'll be dealing with the bride's erratic emotions, family members that don't agree and a groom that just doesn't want to choose a linen color, you're absolutely correct. Therefore, be prepared to become their psychiatrist.

Put yourself in your clients' shoes and walk in the front door of your office. Sometimes we have tunnel vision, so take a look around. Is your office inviting? Does it have an odor? Is it clean (bathrooms too)? If your shop is unorganized, messy and could use a vacuum, then your client may assume that their wedding may be the same way. You can't take back a first impression.

For the first meeting, most couples expect an inviting meeting space, refreshments, photos and background music. Your bride may be meeting you after work and may be stressed out. Slow the pace and offer a glass of wine, cocktail or cup of coffee with a few snacks. After all, we are in the hospitality business.

Yes, it is a different and highly evolved wedding world out there and you have to be many things to your couples. Most brides remember their wedding day as one of the best days of their life – and also the most stressful. This doesn't have to be the case when dealing with you and your company! It's understandable for the bride to feel like she's floundering. Between blogs, articles and Pinterest, she is overwhelmed with planning the wedding of her dreams, but there are ways to make sure that the months leading up to it are as stress-free as possible for the bride and you.

4 Tips for stress free wedding planning:

1. Stay connected to the bride – After booking the event send her a detailed "next steps" outlining how the planning process will work, the number of meetings and what is discussed at each meeting. Include deadline dates for guest count, linen/ rentals, deposits, timeline etc. This drastically reduces the 2AM texts, emails and phones calls when these things pop in the brides mind.

2. Make her feel important - there is nothing more irritating to a bride then having to track you down. Return her calls, emails and texts promptly even if you say you're at an event now but you'll call back at 7:00. Be proactive instead of reactive, set a schedule to call the bride for the "just checking in." She will be very appreciative.

3. Every bride wants to provide sumptuous food at her wedding, and yet catering is one thing that can go disastrously wrong. Miscommunications with your team may result in unreliable service staff and an underwhelming menu that differs from what was promised – these could be incredibly stressful setbacks. It is key that you take detailed notes to enable successful execution of the event. Write down everything, the chef does not read minds.

4. Prevent the last minute panic – Nothing can break the mood of her wedding day pampering like a frantic series of calls from confused vendors. Compile a list of contacts with the set up details, arrival times and flow and provide this to all vendors in the weeks leading up to the day. This way, YOUR massage or work out before set up won't be spoiled.

What a bride really wants is to like you, trust you, believe you and have confidence in you. If you connect with the bride and groom's emotional as well as practical needs, they won't be able to get married without you and that's money in the bank.

CHAPTER 7

SELL EXPERIENCES, NOT THINGS

Most businesses struggle with the dilemma of their company's features and benefits. The sales mantra states that we must sell benefits, not features. Companies speak about Features & Benefits often; however, do you really understand the benefits of your company? When communicating what you offer you'll need to be able to define them clearly. When I visited a catering company last month I asked the sales people to list their company's features. Without missing a beat, they all chimed in and said, *'we have great food, we pay attention to detail. Our service is top notch. Our chef is wonderful'* and so on. Then I asked them *'what are the benefits of using your company?'* They paused for a moment and then repeated the features they gave me earlier. They assumed that having great food is a benefit to their clients. But is it? Most sales people don't really understand the difference between features and benefits. Features tell, benefits sell!

Let me tell you a story that makes this come to life. I was walking through Nordstrom's department store into the mall. A red dress caught my attention; so I made a beeline over there and just fell in love with it. It was so me. With excitement, I took it off the rack, turned it around, then I looked at the price tag - $650! Ouch! Back on the rack it went. As I was leaving the mall, I passed the stunning red dress again. I paused and thought *"It won't hurt if I just try it on"*, so I headed to the dressing room. Wow! The dress looked so amazing. It fit me perfectly. I felt that it complemented my coloring and it made me look slim. I just had to have it! I bought the dress! What happened here? I normally would not spend that much money on an everyday dress but then, the dress made me feel good. Now, let's assume there were two red dresses, one for $650 and another for $350. They may seem similar, so naturally I would want to go for the cheaper one. And then I try them on, feeling elated and beautiful in the $650 dress, while the $350 dress looked just OK, giving me no special feeling whatsoever. Definitely I would opt for the $650 dollar dress that made me look slim and fit and gave me confidence.

Features: Red Dress, Silk

Benefits: Evokes emotion, it made me look slim and fit. It made me feel wonderful. It gave me confidence in my appearance.

This speaks volumes about the sales process. Think back a moment, have you bought something that was more money than you wanted to spend? Chances are the answer is yes!

You most likely have had cause to say these words - *'I didn't book it, our price was too high'* – frustrated after preparing a painstaking proposal for a client only to be turned away for our rates. While we know we are charging a reasonable amount for top-notch service and outstanding results, the client opts for a cheaper – and or less qualified competitor. In order to find out more about this issue, I sent a survey to 474 event professionals around the country- both large & small - and asked them to rank the reasons why they believe that a client didn't book with their company. Here is the result:

Survey

Rank client reasons for not booking event

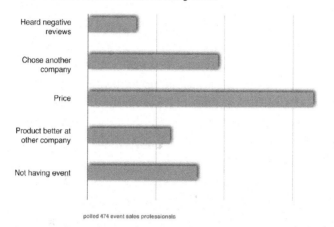

polled 474 event sales professionals

The majority believed they didn't book the event because their price was too high. No! You didn't book it because the client didn't see a difference between your company and your competitor. Remember, features TELL while benefits SELL. Think of it this way, a client requests information from two DJ's one quote was $1200 and the other quote $1500 they look like they are providing the same service no naturally the client will go with the cheaper price. The $1500 DJ did not show the client why they were different and didn't explain the true benefits of using their company I also asked those polled if they could list 5 benefits their clients would derive by using their company, and 98% of the time I got at least three of these answers:

1. Our service is amazing.
2. Our product is fabulous.
3. We've been in business for ___ years.

4. We pay attention to detail.

5. We can work within your budget.

This always makes me wonder – if 98% are saying the same thing, then what sets you apart, and how are you different? You're not. Your client is so accustomed to hearing these phrases from all of the businesses they deal with, and so these features just don't mean anything to them. You are setting yourself up to be a boring old commodity, but you do know there are countless differences between you and your competitors. Those lists above? They simply state the features of your company. You need to emphasize your benefits. A benefit is how your product makes someone *feel* - it evokes an emotion in their world. You simply need to take your company's features and turn them into benefits. Let's use everyone's favorite blonde, Barbie as an example!

Barbie doll's features:

- Style-able hair
- Bendable arms and legs
- Changeable wardrobe
- Makeup can be applied

Benefits:

Let's say you told the potential buyer, *'Can you imagine your daughter sitting on the floor brushing and braiding Barbie's hair into all different styles?'* What do you think the mother is feeling? This image will first bring a smile to her face, evoke love for her daughter and then trigger the realization that, *'Oh good, she'll be busy playing with Barbie so it gives me more time to work!'* With that emotional statement, you have turned a feature into a benefit.

Benefits are the reasons why clients buy your services. One way you can decipher if it's a feature, or a benefit is to ask yourself if it is a fact or a feeling. Every one of your company's features can be turned into a benefit with a little practice. Gather your team and try this exercise that will assist you in realizing the distinction between features and benefits. List a feature, then follow up with a benefit and lastly, how that benefit makes you feel. This way;

Feature- Stunning decor
Benefit- The room will be so beautiful **which means** your event will be all over Instagram
Feeling- 'I would love my event on Instagram'

Feature- Great service, our staff ratio is 10 to 1
Benefit- Our service team is skilled, friendly and efficient, **which means** that your guests won't have to wait in line at the bar for a drink at the reception."
Feeling- 'Oh, I don't want that, that would be embarrassing. I didn't even know that that could be an issue.'

Feature – Delicious food
Benefit – "Our food is fabulous and trend setting **which means** you'll be the envy of all of your friends."
Feeling- 'That would be great. I do want my party to be topnotch'.
Secretly, every wedding, corporate event, house party wants their event to be better than their friends'.

Whether consciously or unconsciously, your clients will continually ask the questions *'What's in it for me?' 'How will I benefit?'* You have to deliver solutions and satisfy their needs.

As much as we would like to believe that our clients are solely buying from our companies for service and experience, they are truly buying based on the way it makes them feel. There is no doubt they have an emotional investment in the decision process. Benefits are so much more evocative and meaningful than the features. Ensure that you are doing your best to transform simple descriptions into client-winning benefit statements!

CHAPTER 8

WHY ARE MY COMPETITORS BUSIER THAN I AM?

The **POWER** of **NETWORKING**

It's not **WHAT** you know- It's **WHO** you know

Perhaps you have found yourself asking that question? Let's think about this for a minute. First time clients who are also using an event planner, photographer or caterer or *(insert what you do here)* for the first time – what in-depth knowledge do they have about your role except that they want to have a special event? In their eyes, a DJ is a DJ, a caterer is a caterer, and all in the same line do the same thing. It is your role as a professional in your line to educate them that we *aren't* all the same. But how? At a conference, a woman approached me and said, *"I just don't get it, I know my product and service is much better than my competitor, but I don't even get a chance to bid on these events."* Why? Because these new clients don't know *anything* about you, let alone that you are the better. Keep in mind that people oftentimes want to work with people they know. There are trust and confidence factors that can't be ignored. You need to join industry and social organizations in your region, get involved, attend meetings, volunteer on committees. I know it's hard and who has time, but put yourself out there and participate. As a new business owner in the late 80's I went to my first Business Card Exchange. With a large stack of business cards in hand, I nervously approached a group of people, stuck out my business card and introduced myself. They were polite, introduced themselves and carried on their conversation. Clearly, I was not part of that conversation and later saw the business cards that I had given them on a table, just discarded. Frustrated, I went to the bar to grab a drink. This nice guy approached me, offered his hand and business card and said, *"Hi, I'm John, I'm a DJ"* Great. This is exactly how I thought a business card exchange should be. We both observed the group from afar and I said to John, *"They aren't even talking about business."* He responded, *"No, they never do. It's just one large clique, like in high school."* Then it hit me. These people were friends and friends not only like to socialize with each other, they also like to work with each other. I don't know where John is today. I don't even think he is still in business, but I owe John a big thank you, because that night I finally understood the power of networking.

Networking

- Join committees- boards
- Don't fear the big shots, introduce yourself
- Keep connected
- Remember the details- google

It's all about the relationship!

Networking is a great way to build a sustainable business. The benefits cannot be over-emphasized. You get to expand your knowledge, learn from others, get referrals to acquire new clients and tell other people about your company. The saying *'It's not what you know, It's who you know'* is very true in the events business. To be successful in the events industry, you need to have a source of relevant connections. The referrals you get through networking are usually high-quality ones and often times even pre-qualified for you. By networking, you are increasing your visibility and raising your profile. Being around people with similar interests and in the same industry as you, stands you in good stead to receive advice. You can readily tap into the expertise of other people with more experience; start relationships that can lead to strategic alliances and joint ventures. You learn about current trends in the industry, this no doubt gives you an edge over your competition. I could go on and on, the benefits of networking are numerous.

Networking shouldn't stop with industry events. Via networking you establish a set of connections that come into play in all aspects of life – not just business. Think about it. We are a service industry. At some point, these "connections" will need our services for their own celebrations. And their friends' celebrations. And the circle just gets wider. It's so easy for us to have tunnel vision. We go on with our busy schedules, trying to balance work and family. It is easy to blow off these meetings when they eat into the little free time we have. But once you make the commitment you will see that it was time well spent to get those invaluable word of mouth referrals. Sell yourself first and in turn the company will sell itself. Remember: The moment you engage with someone, they are judging YOU first, then they're judging what they're buying and then they're judging the company!

CHAPTER 9

PROPS THAT POP

It's not just enough to network; crafting a winning proposal is also essential to booking the event. Your **proposal should pop!** Here's the scenario. It's Friday afternoon and an event planner calls looking for a proposal for a client. She wants it emailed by 10 AM Monday. Yours will be one of the three she will present to her client. And there's the rub – she's doing the presentation, not you. So how are you going to make your voice heard at the pitch meeting? With a proposal that is so striking and imaginative the other two just fade away. Be it a six figure-wedding or a low-budget event down your street, it all starts with a proposal that describes the event. If you're in the events business, you must be able to sell your skills to the client by way of a well-written event proposal. The first step in writing the winning proposal involves having a conversation or researching about the client to find out what she hopes to accomplish at the upcoming event. A proposal is the most client-centric document that your company can create. Each proposal must be designed to suit each client's needs. The best proposals, regardless of the industry follow a similar structure, including the cover page, credentials, and summary of the client's needs, services provided and pricing.

It is very crucial that the proposal you write is relevant to the client. The client is getting proposals from other companies apart from yours; as such it is vital that you don't make the client feel like a commodity. Personalize the proposal. The title of the proposal is very important. When you use a personalized title like *'Jane & Jack Take the Plunge* (bride mentioned that in conversation) versus *Jane & Jack's Wedding*, it shows that you are tailoring the event to the client and not just treating the client like a commodity. While everyone else is naming their proposal with the event name and date, look for ways to stand out by sending a strong message even before the client opens the proposal. Think differently!

To craft a proposal that pops, you should know the client's wishes. During your initial meeting with the client, be sure to take notes besides the time, date, and location for the event. Listen to the client's ideas for issues pertaining to the theme, color scheme and other aesthetic elements of the event. Your proposal should speak directly to the client and their needs. The client needs to feel that their needs are understood. Keep in mind that the client may also be reviewing proposals from other companies offering similar services to yours and is likely to pick the one that best understands their needs.

In designing a proposal, you should include a brief introduction of you and your company. This gives the client an idea of who you are and how long you've been in business. Your proposal should contain a summary of the client's needs and goal for the event. Be sure to go over what the client told you about the event as regards dates, time, proposed venue, theme and other information earlier provided, showing that you understand what they are looking for.

In a proposal, the most important word is 'YOU', that is the client's name. The proposal needs to be client-centric, being about meeting the client's needs. The client basically wants to know how you can help them run an amazing event. Prove how you are going to do this by setting the stage and telling the story. Let's say you're a caterer and your proposal tells this story: *"As guests arrive they ascend the grand staircase to the balcony where our staffs greet them with smiles, champagne and scrumptious hors d'oeuvre artfully presented with river rocks & reeds on stylish polished aluminum salvers"*. By doing this, you are putting the client in the scene and feeding their imagination. Proposals must be tailored to the client's needs in order to make a winning impression. Employ creativity. Who wouldn't rather eat *'seared garlic and lime scented tenderloin skewers'* than *'filet kabobs'*? And if those skewers are staged *'in a jewel box with a flashy orchid'*, they taste even better! Your choice of words matter. Especially for those in the catering line, with food there are so many "yummy" words. Put the reader in the scene by painting mental images. Describe the design elements of your tablescapes with evocative words and photos. As they read, the client will become more and more immersed in the vision you have designed. It's not just *'a vase of red tulips.'* It's *'a glass cylinder enveloped in birch bark bursting with scarlet French tulips.'* Pepper the proposal with buzzwords that relate to the client or event. Let's say you're catering for an electric power company dinner. You could use words like amps, grid or wired for a clever tie-in. Clients like a witty phrase here and there if it fits. Choice of words matter, regardless of your role in the events industry, be sure to use words that bring what you do to life when you write your proposals.

Our client wants to know what services you will be rendering during the event. Say you're into event planning and the upcoming event is large, such as a wedding with many aspects, it might be appropriate to create headings such as "Cocktail Party" or "Luncheon," and then describe the duties you will perform for that aspect of the event – such as setting up the tables and serving food. Add photos of similar events that you've handled in the past to this section of the proposal. This gives the client a vivid example of what you will do.

You've described the event, using language that enables the client to picture the event more vividly. Now, the client is thinking, *'Beautiful, how much is this going to cost?'* In the proposal, create a section titled 'Cost Summary' or 'Proposed Costs' or even 'The Nitty Gritty', listing the prices for each item and their purpose to eliminate ambiguity. Tally them up and write the proposed total event cost. In times past, it used to be selling dreams and charging what you want. Long gone are those days. Given the current economic conditions, most clients are taking a closer look and thinking, "bargain". It is thus beneficial to give the client a choice on pricing or different packages to choose from. Don't just give the client the stated proposed cost or nothing because the client can easily choose nothing and move on to the next vendor who offers similar service for a lesser price. Endeavor to give the client three price points. List the priciest option first so that if the client will have a *'Wow! That is expensive'* reaction, it will be to your most expensive option. They will then see the other pricing options as much more reasonable. It may be advantageous to offer some discount, like a discount for booking early or a package discount for many events booked at the same time. Ensure that you provide your full contact information on every page so the client can contact you again. Too often the client prints all proposals and if your information is not on every page it will get lost in the shuffle.

You don't need special software to make proposal magic. A word doc will work just fine. Save time by saving descriptions in a folder for easy cut and paste or drop-in. And when your kick-ass proposal is ready, make sure you PDF it before sending. Trite but true – you don't get a second chance to make a first impression!

CHAPTER 9

ESSENTIAL SKILLS

9 Essential **Selling** Skills

every sales person must know

Research
prospects and
organizations prior to first

Ask
questions and listen
more than you talk

Focus
on a few top prospects
and contacting them
frequently

Solving
problems and overcoming
objections

5

Creating
long-term relationships
with prospects and clients

Follow up
follow up follow up

Recognizing
when the client is ready
to buy

8

Knowing
how to close the sale
at the right time

9

Getting
referrals and then following
up on them

CHAPTER 10

IDENTIFYING BUYING SIGNALS AND CLOSING THE SALE

When a sales prospect has made the decision to book you, they can sometimes express their desire subtly. This expression could be verbal or non-verbal; in form of a change in their tone of speech or body movements. To effectively identify buying signals, you should be able to listen and watch out for cues that indicate the prospect's interest. A good salesperson must be able to make out subtle buying signals to know when to close the sale. Cues shown by the prospect can be either verbal or non-verbal. Often times, a client will show repeated patterns of verbal and non-verbal cues, thus a noticeable shift in the patterns can indicate a change in attitude.

Body Language

55% of All Human Communication is Nonverbal

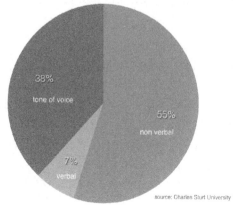

38%
tone of voice

55%
non verbal

7%
verbal

source: Charles Sturt University

Verbal cues refer to the prospect's words. Buying signals can take on the form of statements or questions from the prospect. A passive client who suddenly begins to ask questions or shedding more light about their needs is verbally showing you signs of interest. You should listen to what the client is saying and how they are saying it. Verbal cues go a long way in telling you what the client wants. A client who is confiding in you and telling you about issues experienced with past vendors or asking you questions on clients you have worked with on similar events is signaling her interest. It shows that there is a level of rapport and the client has a measure of confidence, all that is needed is a nudge from you in the right direction. Buying signals can show up at any time in a meeting with a client. It's up to you to recognize these signals so that you can react accordingly and move towards the close when it's most suitable to do so. Statements like these could indicate a client's interest in booking you or buying from you;

- *'Are there any other styles or colors to choose from?'*
- *'How much money do you need to start?'*
- *'Do I have to pay it all right now or can I do it in installments?'*
- *'Do you offer any other discounts?'*

Non-verbal cues refer to the client's body language, voice inflection and tone of voice. Did you know that 55% of all human communication is non-verbal? Non-verbal expressions provide you insight into the attitude of the client. By being attentive to these cues, you decipher the client's feelings. Some general guidelines for body language cues frequently experienced during sales interactions are the following:

- Uneasiness or suspicion: Clearing throat, picking at skin or clothing, averted gaze, hands covering mouth, rubbing nose or eyes, crossed arms, turning aside or moving away from you

- Frustration or defensiveness: Crossed legs and arms, sighing or huffing, running hand through hair or rubbing back of neck

- Interest or evaluation: Tilting head, removing or peering over eyeglasses, stroking chin, hand on bridge of nose

- Distraction or disinterest: Staring, doodling, drumming, attending to something else, head resting in palm

- Agreement or cooperation: Sitting on edge of chair, leaning forward, open arms and hands, touching gestures, unbuttoning coat

- Uncertainty or doubt: Touching or chewing pen, rubbing thumbs together, shaking head

- Confidence or trust: Straight back, smiling, preening

A measure of intuition and interpersonal skills will help you to recognize and interpret a client's feelings. Be vigilant to recognize a change especially in non-verbal cues. For instance, a client who has been leaning back in her chair all the while suddenly leans towards you; this shift is body language signals an interruption in the client's thought process or change in attitude. It is critical that you take time to recognize a client's readiness to buy. No matter how competent you are, if you don't develop skills in recognizing buying signals and closing the deal, your career in the events industry will suffer. Many salespeople make the mistake of selling themselves right out of a sale! If you don't pay enough attention to recognize the buying signals, you could miss the window of opportunity when the prospect is most receptive to booking you. Pick up the buying signals, and then move to close the sale!

CHAPTER 11

YOU'RE NOT SELLING IF YOU'RE NOT CLOSING

One of the most crucial stages of selling is **closing the sale**. You're not selling if you're not closing the sale! Closing can be scary. Finally, that moment of truth when you find out if you're going to book the event or not! In the sale process, you should discover the client's needs and effectively communicate how your products or services provide a solution to the client's needs. If you achieve these two, then there should be no obstacle to closing the deal. Sometimes the client closes the deal for you. Best-case scenario. At other times, you would need to move to close the deal yourself. It is very important that you develop your closing skills. Sales materials like brochures, flyers and social media marketing can spark an interest in the client and help you start a dialog with the client; the client books after they have discussed their needs with you, seen that they trust and have confidence in you to help them achieve their goal of an amazing event. When closing the sale, don't push to close too soon. Asking for a close too early makes you seem pushy. There's a natural point in a conversation where you know it's time to close. If you continue the conversation beyond that natural point, you risk raising issues that did not exist before. There are many strong ways to close a deal; here are some lines for closing;

- *'Shall I move forward and confirm this on our calendar?'*

- *'I am so excited we'll be working together'*

- *'I can't wait to see this all come together, let's get it on the books''*

Don't begin implementing your ideas for an event without getting the client to sign. If a client has said *'yes'* to working with you, ensure you document the decision. Let's assume you are nearing the end of the selling cycle. Your client has the proposal and is satisfied with the price and certainly likes you. You ask the client for the sale and they say that they need to think about it a little more. Think about it? What more can you do? At that time it is important to ask this question exactly, "what is your hesitation?" They will indeed answer this question. It could be as simple as they didn't like the floor plan or as complicated as we're just not sure. The floor plan you can easily fix but if your client is "not sure" or needs to think about it more then you did not do a good job in selling. You will need to start from the beginning because somewhere along the way you did not make them feel that they are confident in your or the company.

If your client states that they love everything but needs to speak to their boss or attend a meeting with another company, that is understandable. However, don't let them go just yet. Offer your client an Express Refund. Have them give you a deposit at that time and give them time to talk to their boss or attend the other meeting. If at that time they do not want your services you promptly return the deposit.

BOOKED IT!

Express Refund Form

Since we can't guarantee that your date will remain open we
recommend locking into your date with a $_____**Deposit.**
Because we realize this is a big decision we offer a grace period.

If you change your mind by _____ we will return your deposit, in
full promptly. This way you have the security of knowing you have
your date while you're confirming your decision.

After you explain the Express Refund you must leave the room. You need to give the client time to discuss this with one another. Think of it when you buy a car with your spouse. You chat before opening the door to the dealership that you are just looking and not buying today. You like the car and you're in the salespersons office going over numbers. Then the salesperson states that he may be able to lower the price a bit but he needs to talk to the manager. He leaves the room. This gives the couple a chance to agree that it is a good deal. Don't forget the couple agreed that they were just looking, so it is important that they have a conversation to break their deal. That is why car salespeople leave the room. They are not going to talk to the manager- they know the margins exactly.

Keep in mind these 5 easy-to-follow rules on closing the sale;

Rule 1 – Treat closing as a process
Rule 2 – Set an appropriate closing objective
Rule 3 – Let close emerge from conversation
Rule 4 – Wait for the right moment
Rule 5 – Celebrate your success

Don't forget to ask for a referral but remember you only earn the right to ask for a referral after the client is delighted by what was sold to them.

CHAPTER 12

PROACTIVE SALES

In today's event industry, you can't just afford to sit back passively and hope all day that clients will come knocking. The market is competitive and getting new clients can be quite a challenge. This is all the more so because potential clients have many alternatives in regards of who to book. The event industry is a large and constantly growing one. The increase in the number of competitors, the channels through which they can be accessed and the wide ranges of services they offer all give the potential client a variety of options. Besides this, winning on price has become more challenging; your competitors are able to match price offerings. This means there is a need to differentiate your own offering in alternative ways. Keeping this mind, you can't afford to take a laid back approach to client acquisition. To make headway in the competitive events industry, you must take to the streets, literally. The proactive pursuit of prospects should be incorporated into your company's sales strategy and reflect in your activities. Proactive sales is the process of selecting high potential clients and giving such clients intensive sales focus. Proactive sales involve planning for sales growth. To engage in proactive sales, commitment is essential to success.

To sell proactively, you have to bring together all the resources your company has and leverage those resources to create competitive advantage, you should offer solutions to the prospective client's needs and grab opportunities to exceed their expectations. There is a huge difference between being proactive and being reactive. Many of us are fantastic at being reactive. In reactive sales, there is extensive reliance on word-of-mouth, advertising and promotions. You then wait for the client to make the move, that is, visit your office or give you a phone call like an order taker. Proactive sales, on the other hand, involves actively pursuing prospects, this could be through emails, cold calling and visits. In this approach, you find out the needs of your potential clients, match your products and services to potential clients before you make a visit, with a well prepared pitch.

Calling on potential clients is one of the most important activities for a proactive seller. Unless you have spent several years building up an enormous client base that keeps producing referrals, you have to go after prospects and work on client acquisition. To be proactive, it is vital that you schedule time each day to qualify new prospects, set initial appointments and keep in touch with other prospective clients. Proactive sales techniques include identifying the right prospects by means of lead generation, making use of directories, and networking extensively. Keep your eyes and ears open. Is there a new Mercedes dealer or shopping center opening in the area? They will likely have a grand opening launch event. Read the local newspaper and watch the daily news, you may hear of a gala taking place or a new business coming to your market that you can target for next year. The events industry has many professional associations and organizations that you can get involved with. These provide opportunities to meet and interact with other events professionals. You can identify the right prospects via industry events and referrals, and then qualify them before making the initial call or visit. Actively contact organizations, and even other businesses that may need your services. Go out and create opportunities! I think the easiest way to increase your sales goal is to simply ask your current clients if they would mind doing an email introduction to a friend or colleague that may be interested in your services. People like to help others. What's the worst that could happen? The client may say that they don't know of anyone. But, the odds are in your favor. You can sit all day and recite fancy slogans but that is what it all boils down to, just fancy slogans. To be successful, you need to be able to create opportunities and take advantage of opportunities when available. The reason many people never make it is because they have not acted on opportunities available to them. One saying I like is, *"Failing to plan is planning to fail."* Keeping that saying in mind helps you to keep your thinking cap on.

> # If you fail to plan, you'll plan to fail.

> – Benjamin Franklin

When meeting people and selling to them, there are nine essential skills sales people should keep in mind. These include researching prospects and organizations prior to first contact, asking questions and listening, focusing on a few top prospects and contacting them frequently, solving problems and overcoming objections, creating long-term relationships with prospects and clients, communicating appropriate messages, recognizing when the client is ready to buy, knowing how to close the sale at the right time, getting referrals and following up on them.

CHAPTER 13

STATEGIC UPSELLING

What is Strategic Upselling?

Strategic selling involves increasing your competitive advantage by strengthening your ability to **communicate your uniqueness**, value and competitive differential to a customer or prospect.

You are NOT a Commodity

A major sales strategy for more profit is **Strategic upselling**. Right now, I'm sure you're thinking *'How could I possibly increase my sales volume when clients continue to tighten their spending?'* Oh, but you can! There's no secret to upselling – it's merely a sales strategy. As a matter of fact upselling is the quickest and easiest way to increase your sales. Keep in mind that upselling can on the average boost sales by 20 to 42 percent, simply by asking your own version of *'Want fries with that?'* Here are some upselling techniques:

- **Put an upsell right on your proposal.** This method is one of the easiest and most profitable techniques you can start implementing immediately. At the end of the proposal, add a few sentences about some cool ideas you have. It can be something as simple as a signature beverage, late night bites or ambience lighting. You can expect to get a 25 percent upsell rate on average. That means one out of every four clients will give you more money just for adding a few words onto your proposal.

- **Silently selling while meeting with the client.** This is handled a few different ways. If the client meeting is in your office make sure you have good quality photographs hung on the walls, looping on your iPad or photo album opened. Remember, humans are visual and images appeal a lot to the senses. If your client ordered standard linens, have a few gorgeous upgraded linens in the event theme just lying around. Take your client on a tour of your shop. Something will catch their eye and they will want to add it to the event. You get the picture.

- **Customers who bought this also bought this.** In my opinion, Amazon is the master of the upsell. How difficult would it be to have a few proposals of other events in actual client files (black out names) to show your client? People are always curious of what others have chosen at their events. You will notice a significant increase in sales.

- **New and different.** One of my favorites is contacting the client out of the blue and letting them know that you just saw in a magazine or conference something brand new on the market and you thought of them first.

They'll be flattered that you were thinking about their event and who doesn't want something new and different.

Effective upselling strategies

Assumption is the key!

Leader Proposal

Training the salesperson

You can incorporate in your daily

schedule

Decide what you will upsell/cross sell

Be warned however, upselling can back fire. Keep it simple, complicated offers confuse customers. Don't oversell your products or services and most importantly know when a client really means no. Develop a company-wide sales plan that you can incorporate in your daily schedule that includes 6 to 10 products or services. Integrate procedures you will take to implement an effective upselling blueprint. Strategic upselling involves increasing your competitive advantage by strengthening your ability to **communicate your uniqueness**, value and competitive differential to the client. The key to successful upselling is to train sales people to focus their efforts on meeting the clients' needs not just to sell more stuff. By doing this, you will increase your margins and build client loyalty.

CHAPTER 14

KICK STARTING YOUR SALES; AND YOUR PASSION

It happens to the best of us – you get into a slump, your state of mind is a bit "blah" and your creativity wanes. Perhaps your bookings start to drop off, and you find yourself struggling to hit sales targets that you used to breeze right past. Does any of this sound familiar? You most definitely need to kick-start your sales and get some fresh perspective, ideas, and motivation. If you continue to do things the same way you always have, you can't be surprised if you don't see any new results. Don't be afraid to try new things—rekindle your passion in sales and you will see results. Here are seven ideas to get you back in gear.

Don't be afraid to try new things - rekindle your passion in sales and you will see results. Here are a few tips on reviving sales.

- **Social Media**

Social networking websites give individuals and businesses the opportunity to relate with one another and build online communities. Consumers can interact directly with companies when companies join social channels, with the interaction being more personal to users than traditional methods of outbound marketing and advertising. Social media is one of the most powerful tools at any sales person's disposal - you'd be surprised that by being active on social media, you can increase your sales. Social media is a fun, informal space for you to talk to your clients, reaching out to them like they are your personal friends. Avoid "posting and boasting," and instead explain *why* you like a particular event, *how* excited you are about planning a party or *share* an interesting cooking method. People will get turned off if you're just sharing, liking or retweeting a link from your company. Bring your personality to the table and you will be amazed at how well people respond.

- **Sell Yourself**

Your food may be delicious, you may be an incredible baker and your reviews fantastic, but without an effective branding strategy that sells **who you are**, you are sure to get lost in the sea of competitors. People want to do business with a face and a name that they can relate to – highlight your unique qualities, competencies, wealth of experience, and like-minded clients will follow.

• Get organized

This may seem like a no-brainer, but it is so vital to your success. Productivity is all about being efficient, that is doing more, and faster too. Managing your workspace and time is crucial to improving your productivity. De-clutter your desk (and your inbox) - you'd be surprised on what you'd find. No, not chocolate (although, yum!). You may find a lost inquiry or notes from a meeting with a bride last week. By organizing your tasks, you will be able to prioritize and focus on more important things. Keep tabs on communication – emails, files, letters, to-do lists, status reports. Another helpful organizational tip I have found beneficial is planning the upcoming week the Thursday before; don't start planning your week on Monday. Plan beforehand. It pays to write down exactly what you want to achieve with deadlines. Deadlines force productivity. Deadlines are the friends of accomplishment. So often we get interrupted and lose focus, as such it is vital to keep a daily list of your activities.

• Compete with yourself

For many people, competition is a motivator, and competing with your own past results is a great way to get your blood pumping and your business booming. Staying worried about a competitor's ability can be self-defeating and counter-productive. It is vital to build on your fundamental capabilities to learn, relate, act and re-invent yourself. Strive for self-improvement and be better than you were yesterday. What better way to do this than to set goals and work towards achieving them? Set monthly, quarterly and annual goals to ensure that your business is always growing.

- **Know thyself.**

What's your skill set? What can you offer a client that no one else can? Step back and think of all the things that you're good at in the sales process - you may be fabulous in bonding with the client but poor in qualifying them, and therefore lose opportunities. Once you identify your strengths and weaknesses you can work on the areas that you need to improve.

- **Showcase your success**

Whenever you get publicity, you could reprint articles containing the publicity and mail such with sales letters, fliers or any other marketing literature that you use to advertise your company. Doing this back up the claims that you make for your company. It tells clients and prospects that they are dealing with a reputable company. Showcasing your achievements, laurels and positive testimonies will help the client feel more confident when they decide to book you. When meeting with prospects, present the right image. Words of caution however; ensure you don't overdo this. Cockiness can be annoying.

- **Take time to build relationships**

Sales success goes beyond the 1st event. You invested a lot of time cultivating a client bond, and now you need to continue the relationship after the event. Ask them for referrals and find out if their employer, friends and family need your expertise. Maintaining these long-term relationships is vital in sales. It is easy to dismiss existing relationships as a key strategy. Satisfied customers are good marketing tools. These people through their experience will be willing to share positive testimonies and tell good stories about your company and your services to other people. Don't be afraid to ask for referrals. Contacting organizations, schools and even other businesses that may need your services is a great marketing strategy. Talk to people from whom you buy your own products, hand out your business cards. They just might be in need of your services or know someone who does.

Remember, if you are struggling to kick-start or revive your sales, you're not alone. The struggle to make your company the best it can be and continue on an upward trajectory is one that every sales person faces, but by remembering your passion and trying new things, you will see results. Even the best salespeople can get better and high performing teams can sharpen their focus. A regular sales checkup is critical to assessing and addressing the strengths, weaknesses and opportunities of your sales efforts. This should entail an inclusive step-by-step system from initial inquiry to closing the sale.

CHAPTER 15

GET MOTIVATED!

Slumps in your level of motivation are a natural phenomenon. Lack of motivation however, can have dire financial consequences such as reduction in profit. Motivated sales people sell more, no doubt. Going about your business looking like the weight of the world is on your shoulders has never helped anyone boost their sales. Attitude and mindset play significant roles in enabling you to reach targets and shoot your company to the heights you desire.

Complacency is the enemy of success. It is easy to become complacent over time, never pushing oneself and ceasing to go an 'extra mile' for the sake of your company and clients. Without doubt, you know that you need to be motivated in order to succeed at sales, you want to be motivated but you find out that you just cannot attain and maintain that motivation. Is this the case? Motivation is an in-house job; it begins and ends with you. Even if you fail to realize it, motivation is something you can control, an internal job. No one gets to determine your level of motivation. You need to take responsibility for your motivation – every second, every minute, hourly and daily. While it is good to source for inspiration from motivational speakers, workshops and mantras, the drive to increase sales must come from within you. Rekindling motivation starts with bearing in mind the reason why you started your company in the first place. Doubts and other issues can make you lose sight of why you started and your initial passion. It is passion for what you do and an unreserved belief in what you're selling that drives you to win clients over at the end of the day. Review the thank-you letters, calls, publicity and awards you have received from satisfied clients and rekindle that passion for what you do! It goes a long way in renewing your enthusiasm for selling.

Motivating a team is one of the most important things that a leader can do. Without guidance, employees can flail and suffer, unsure of what to do next and how to succeed to their highest potential. While it is true that no one can truly motivate anyone (true gumption has to come from within), a good leader can do a tremendous amount to influence people and encourage their motivation and success.

COMPLACENCY—THE ENEMY OF A SUCCESSFUL TEAM

Part of keeping your team motivated and excited about always improving is also ensuring that they don't become complacent. We all know the type: arrive to work in a daze, clock in, and then sit at their desk doing the bare minimum to get by. Then, they leave as early as possible, never really committing to their career path, and worst of all—detract from, rather than add to, the success of the team. If these types are already satisfied with what they have, it can become increasingly difficult to engage them and motivate them to success.

Why do good people become complacent?

Sometimes even the best workers can become complacent over time. Feeling happy and fulfilled in their career, some individuals can fall into the habit of quiet complacency, never pushing themselves and ceasing to go that 'extra mile' for their boss or their client. They do this without realizing that their co-workers and manager may be fostering a slowly simmering resentment toward their blasé attitude.

Are competitions really motivating your team?

Many managers decide to motivate their teams by setting up competitions and monetary incentives intended to encourage everyone to get back on board and do their very best. Team spirit! While these types of incentives can be a temporary measure that appears to work at first, money is not always the answer. Sometimes the very best motivating factors are interpersonal relationships—caring for the success of the team is an excellent way to boost morale and performance.

Focus on relationships with your team

We all know what it feels like to be managed skillfully versus being managed poorly. If you are in management, know that trying to intimidate your employees into respecting you will not work. A Drill Sargent won't gain their employees' respect.

Instead of barking orders, counteract complacency by celebrating goals and accomplishments. Make a big deal out of it when they make a huge sale or land a new client! By warmly and regularly congratulating your team when they do well (and working on building them up when they are struggling) you will reach goals you have never dreamed of.

Nip negativity: get rid of cancerous employees

Negative employees, or CAVE dwellers (Consistently Against Virtually Everything) are a cancer in your organization. They will bring you down and destroy the morale of your other employees. Sometimes you can work with these individuals in order to get them back on track, but sometimes they just have to go. Conversely, you may have a great employee who just isn't getting the job done, consistently underperforming and bringing the team down. Don't be too quick to dismiss these people—they may simply be in the wrong position in your company. Sit down and ask them, "If I had a magic wand, what position would you like to have in this company?" By listening to your employee you will learn how to better manage them and bring your entire team to success.

Laugh and play with your team!

Most importantly, you have to remember that we are all social beings. Saying thank you and laughing with your team can go much further toward a harmonious and successful business environment than any competition can. Spend time together, enjoy their company, and listen to what they have to say—these are the steps to managing your team with poise, enjoyment, and skill.

CHAPTER 16

GIVE YOUR HOLIDAY SALES MARKETING A NEW RECIPE

As summer winds down and the busy season comes to an end, you have the chance to catch your breath for a few brief moments—and then jump right back in. That's right—it's time to promote your holiday sales!

In order to stand out from the others you need to show that you are different. As business owners we can't just expect revenue to flow our way; we need to compete for the business and prove that we are the best choice for our clients. Following are some tips that will help you stand out from the crowd.

Update your database

You may have thousands of email and postal addresses, but if they are not current your mail outs will fail. Spend some time adding your new clients to your database and updating corporate contacts that may have moved on. (Another thought is to stay connected to individuals who leave your corporate accounts so you are on their minds when they start at their new positions.)

The newsletter no-no

Your newsletter is not the space to promote your holiday events, offerings, and promotions—these beneficial holiday offers may get lost in your newsletter and also dilute your message. Consider a dedicated brochure or mail out in order grab attention.

Tell a story

Your marketing pieces may get some traction if they tell an engaging story—this works well with postcard mailings and social media campaigns. Each ad you create should tell a story or have a theme. Consider creating characters, as this will this leave the audience wanting to know what happens next. (For my company we produced a flutter of children cooking to promote house parties, along with a tag line.)

Cyber Monday

If you do a good amount of online business make sure that you take advantage of Cyber Monday. Consider running 'limited time' specials, or a promotion in which your clients receive a bonus, gift, or discount if they book within a certain time frame.

Decorate for success

You probably decorate your office for the holidays, and so why not decorate your website? Create landing pages with specials, menus, tips, and recipes and spread these to your social media platforms.

Spread some cheer on social media

Your social media platforms are a great way to spread holiday cheer. Be careful not to bore your followers by pushing your product, repeating terms like 'book now,' 'taking reservations,' and 'still have some availability.' These terms are sure to prevent any possibility for sharing—no one wants to repost a sales-forward link. Instead, post genuinely interesting and valuable information and your followers will reciprocate.

Additionally, paid advertising can be a great way to attract new clients and reach different audiences. Why not use this holiday season as a chance to try a Facebook ad campaign?

It's not always about price

Don't worry if your closest competitors are offering lower prices. Studies have shown that clients do not always make their pick based on price; they want the best that they can afford, and are often willing to stretch a budget to get what they want. Become what they want, and show them why you are different.

CHAPTER 17

WHERE HAVE ALL THE FANS GONE? LONG TIME PASSING

Is it bewildering to you that you may have 2000 page likes on your Facebook business page, but when you review the analytics your post views dropped to the double digits? Now that's a head scratcher. Chances are you are feeling discouraged, you're spending many hours keeping your page updated and no one is listening!

When I contacted Facebook, here's what they said "Facebook's engineering team makes changes to the News Feed algorithm to help make Facebook more engaging for people." Then I read an article from AdAge where Facebook openly states that business page owners should expect their organic reach to continue to decline over time... and the best way to get your content seen is to pay for reach. It is obvious that Facebook is training us to buy ads or boost posts. I can understand that, Facebook is a business. However, for those of us that are not a mega company like Target or Lexus that are selling a tangible product, though, you are supplying free content; a recipe, advice, photo inspiration and a blog; this becomes costly. Call me crazy; we're giving free content that we have to pay for. But there is something you can do. Facebook also states: Organic posts from friends that people did not initially see can reappear near the top of News Feed if the stories are still getting likes and comments. This gives the best posts a greater chance of being seen by more people.

Then I dug deeper... In Amy Porterfield's 2015 Guide to Facebook Engagement, Facebook defines engagement in one way and one way only: fingers clicking specific buttons. If a fan doesn't engage with your post in at least one of four ways—like it, leave a comment, share it with others, or click on a link—it's not considered engagement by Facebook standards. Period. So what does non-engagement look like? Here are things that your Facebook fans may be doing that do not count as Facebook engagement:

- Read your update. Kind of makes you rethink how much time you spend crafting the perfect status, doesn't it?

- View your image. Photos, infographics, inspirational quotes, etc. are great ways to grab attention, but simply having them seen does not constitute engagement.

- Click on a photo. If your photo is not linked (via OpenGraph or some other plug-in) to a specific site, all that will happen is that the photo will open in a bigger window. That's an opportunity to giving your reader yet another chance to engage...but in itself; Facebook doesn't count it as fan engagement.

- Like your page. You heard right. People liking your page doesn't affect engagement; it only counts when they like specific posts.

That's how Facebook sees engagement; let's explore what engagement might mean to you. When someone interacts with the content you have posted, they are expressing interest in you. That means your WHY, your meaning, your purpose. What do you do, and how do you do it?

Don't sell yourself short. Your why and how are powerful stuff to people out there. Knowing about you is reward in itself. If you are message driven, sharing what you care about in a true attempt to educate, entertain, or inspire people, and those people communicate back to you or push it out to the world... that is a reflection that you are doing something right!

So Why Does Engagement Matter? This is where mindset enters the picture. Mindset is what will connect the dots for you between fan engagement (likes, comments, shares, and clicks) and exposure to your business (such as getting your posts into your tribe's News Feed). The equation is simple: Boost your engagement (likes, comments, shares, & clicks) and get rewarded.

See, the more often your fans engage with you in the ways listed above, the more often your posts will be pushed out into their News Feed. This is how Facebook helps your business–by noticing that people are interested in what you have to say, and giving them more. Therefore, in each and every status update you post, you'll want to influence your audience to engage in at least one of the four ways that count: liking, commenting, sharing, or clicking a link. This is where your mindset is critical. When you're creating a Facebook post, it's not enough to be clever, or even thoughtful. When you create a Facebook post, you need to come at it this way: "How can I thoughtfully construct this post to ignite the action needed for my fans to engage?"

Remember, if there is no engagement, Facebook simply thinks your audience is not interested. And they're not going to promote something that they think people aren't interested in. On the other hand, the more people take action on one of your posts, the more your posts will show up in their feed. Not just that one post they liked, but all your posts. Say you've been getting lots of "likes" on a particular photo you posted, or had people commenting throughout the week on a status update...and then, later in the week or month, you post something about a specific promotion you're doing. All those likes and comments are what will take your promotional post straight to your fans' News Feed. Simply put, an increase in fan engagement also equals an increase in the exposure of your promotional posts.

Are you beginning to understand the roadmap? As you consistently offer high quality, valuable content that captivates your audience and motivates them to engage, through an indirect process you will increase your sales. It's important for people to engage (like, click, comment, share) with your business' posts to regularly see them in News Feed.

So, engage your fans by:

- Asking Questions- Questions are a great way to spark dialogue with fans. It is probably the easiest way and one of the best methods to get people to respond to your posts.

- Photos- Photos stand out better compared to status updates or posted links. Pictures are clear and concise and are easily palatable to the mind.

- Contests- Contests not only reward loyal fans, but also it creates excitement and will get users to visit your Facebook page frequently to check if they have won.

You need to build that trust, and doing things like sharing valuable content, news articles, and information on the latest and greatest in your industry will prove that your fan base can trust what you say and will come back again and again. And if all else fails, add the Facebook Join My Mailing List App on your business page. The App makes it easier for you to collect new contacts directly from your Facebook fan or business page to use with Constant Contact, Mail Chimp etc.

CHAPTER 18

SELLING YOUR STYLE

A few weeks ago a caterer emailed me and said she is spending a lot of money on decorating her food stations for her events and is not charging the client. I asked why she feels the need to do this. Without pause, she quickly answered, because I want to make sure the food and décor compliment each other. BINGO-She needs to sell her style.

You may already have a brand style if a guest attends your event and knows that your company catered it just by the way it looks. I know a caterer that has the word peach in their name. At *every* event there will be peaches, whether it's a bowl at the buffet or a single peach at the bar. Instant recognition. Another way is to use a few unique pieces that create your signature look.

Selling your style is much easier than you think - you just need the selling tools and a few sales techniques.

Photos Photos Photos - but only high quality photos. Most caterers are too busy setting up and don't have time to take photos at their events. Contact the photographer in advance to take a few detail & room shots. Place your photos on your walls like an art gallery. Creating photo albums that represent your style and digital content in the social media arena is paramount. In this case a picture is worth a 1000 words dollars.

All eyes & ears - You'll get a good sense of your client's style before they utter one word just by looking at them. If a client is wearing floral pastels, with matching nail polish and hair accessories, she is most likely the romantic style. If a client looks like they just walked off a fashion runway, odds are she has a contemporary style.

If you are meeting your client at their home you can determine their style immediately. You may want to suggest their style and the polar opposite in your design pitch for that "I want to do something different". Listen to what your client is saying. Incorporate their ideas into the proposal; most clients need to feel they are part of the design process.

Talk the talk, walk the walk - Old expression yet, current concept. Think about it, you are at the grocery store and notice expired dates, produce looks sparse shriveled and he staff is nowhere to be found. Your internal alarm should be buzzing like crazy. GET OUT. The same concept is for your environment where you meet clients; make sure it's clean, organized and well decorated. Now take a step back and look into the mirror. What does your style say about you: creative, funky, classic, disheveled? It may change the way your clients interact with you.

Show Room - This is essential even if you're in a tight space. Clients are visual. Set up an area with china, glassware, flatware, some linen and chair samples. This is a huge opportunity for you to upsell.

Mood/Inspiration/Story Board - This is a great way to put together a collection of different design styles. Some use their own designs and others will pull from different places. Pintrest certainly has made it very easy to create the boards, just send the client the link!

White Space Design - Tired of hearing, "umm, I don't know, I just can't visualize how it will look." Sometimes photos won't help you sell a design, in catering the client can taste your culinary creations and quickly make a decision. In design it may be a bit more challenging. Create a white space in your office or warehouse. Designate a 10x10 area sectioned out in white pipe & drape creating a white box. This gives you a blank slate to showcase your designs such as a table setting, food station, bar setup etc. Add lighting to complete the look.

CHAPTER 19

FUNDRAISER 101: HELP YOUR CLIENT UNDERSTAND THAT FREE IS NOT FREE

Involved in a small not-for-profit organization? Have you ever raised money for a charity, either at home or abroad? Helped out a local museum or sports team? If you answered 'yes' to any of these, then chances are you have attended – or even helped to organize – a fundraising event. Fundraising events are important for many reasons, and they can prove to be an invaluable tool for anyone hoping to raise money for a good cause.

That said, people are often absolutely inundated by requests to donate their time and money. With the advent of 'crowd funding' these requests have reached a fever pitch, and with a limited amount of donors out there the competition is stiff. Can you help your clients stand out and gain those coveted RSVPs to their event?

Event planners and caterers can help a fundraiser succeed. As an expert in the catering and party planning business, you know better than anyone that fundraising events are a part of our business – but increasingly clients are finding it harder to make their fundraiser stand out, and they want their event planner to wow them with new ideas.

One of the metrics by which to measure a successful fundraiser is repeat attendance – you need to make sure that your fundraiser is amazing so that the guests cannot wait to come back each year. Repeat guests? Repeat donations and a very happy client who is eager to hire you again annually.

Here are some tried and true tips that can help your client plan a fundraiser that they will never forget.

- **Stack your Committee** - Having a large committee may be daunting, but it really is a case of 'bigger is better' when it comes to this aspect. It's important to have heavy hitter names featured - now is the time to name drop (it's not tacky when it's for charity!). My sister lives in Palm Beach and she attends 4-6 fundraisers a month. When the invitation arrives she will often first look at who is on the committee – having a look for friends that she needs to support or a local celebrity she'd like to meet. The lesson is clear - try to get as many heavy hitters as possible on your committee, even if they are there in name only. You can't expect your heavy hitter committee members to carry out committee tasks, make sure you have enough worker bees.

- **Concentrate on a good party – Sit down dinners are a snooze**. Sit down dinner fundraisers can be a bore, and clients are conditioned to expect a cookie cutter event. Now is the time to wow them by planning a great party that leaves guests entertained, engaged and feeling generous. Creative food and drink stations inspired by food trucks, a great band that gets them dancing and plenty of opportunities for networking.

- **Forget about a dinnertime auction – you don't have their full attention.**

    Auctions that take place during a sit down meal have been proven to be less successful than those that take place when attention is undivided. There should be three phases to the event. This is a timeline that has worked for me countless times:

    1. A cocktail reception with heavy passed hors D'oeuvres and well placed bars. This is where the silent auction does best.

    2. Live auction- Hand out customized paddles and usher the guests into a Sotheby's style auction in a separate room – you have their attention, and

bidding is infectious! This should be no more than 45 minutes, and feature big and small ticket items. This phase is where the real money is donated.

3. Open the event back up to a large party with food stations and dancing (remember, you can still sell tables, but this format really increases and encourages mingling and networking).

- **Ticket sales are to cover costs only - they are not a moneymaker.**

Your ticket price should only reflect the costs of the event. If the event is exciting and well-planned the major donations will be made during the fundraiser.

Once your valuable fundraising clients see how successful you have made their event they are likely to come back to you again and again for annual contracts. It is up to you to make your clients' good cause stand out in the sea of fundraisers out there – follow the above tips and you are sure to impress.

CHAPTER 20

The Twelve Components of Sales Excellence in the Special Events Industry

Individuals who enter the special events industry are a unique breed – they have a passion for celebrating the moments in their client's lives with flair and creativity, and they will stop at nothing to ensure that an event or a conference is executed without a hitch. Event pros are passionate and excited about what they do – and they do it well.

With that said, most people involved in the event planning and special event industry entered into this field not because of their skill set in hospitality – but while these elements are vital, they are not the only factors necessary for success. In this industry you must be more than a brilliant caterer and a meticulous planner, you must also have panache for sales.

Sell, plan and execute – are you strong in all three?

In order to succeed and make your business everything you know it can be, you need to be a master at following skills:

- **Selling** – You know that your vision will blow your prospective clients away, but now you just need to convince them to feel the same!

- **Planning** – Meticulous planning involves creativity, attention to detail and the ability to think outside the box. Without confident and effective planning, even if you event is a hit, the stress you have caused your clients (and yourself) will lead to poor reviews and negative word of mouth.

- **Execution** – This is the real test of your mettle. Ensuring that your event is elegant, well received and on trend is the third major responsibility of any successful event planner.

For most people in the special events industry, planning and execution are their strongest suits, and sales can fall by the wayside.

Are your sales skills – or lack there of – hindering your business and preventing you from achieving the heights you could otherwise be reaching? You are not alone. Read ahead for vital sales tips that can help you change the way you operate your business.

Twelve Sales Tips that will change the way you approach sales!

1. **Attitude** – Great sales skills begin with your attitude. Even if you are feeling down, stressed or irritated, you have to let this go and approach every sales meeting with verve and energy. Let your prospective client know just how much their business means to you, and keep that smile on your face. If you enter the meeting feeling defeated, your clients will sense this, and their business will go to a competitor.

2. **Desire** – You know you want this job, your staff members know you want this job, your spouse knows you want this job – now you must communicate this desire to your clients! When they see how excited you are to help them plan their special occasion your excitement will be contagious. Even if another vendor offers them a lower quote, they will remember your desire and passion.

3. **Tenacity** – To be truly tenacious, you need to use new information in order to make new decisions and find new ways to reach your goals. The key word is new! Stay on top of current publications, make new connections and network constantly – these factors will help you with your sales savvy.

4. **Highly motivated by money** - A great salesperson is motivated by their financial rewards at the end of the project. This is where add-ons, special request

fulfillments and accurate billing all come into play –
make sure that you are valuing your time correctly!

5. **Eager to learn -** When it comes to sales – as well as
    most aspects of your career – a hunger for new
    information and a commitment to lifelong learning will
    guarantee that you stay up to date with new skills (and
    sales techniques) that will strengthen your sales
    abilities.

6. **Self-confident -** A great salesperson simply must have
    confidence in their own abilities and the capacity of
    their company to fulfill their clients' requests. If you
    don't believe in yourself, why should your clients?

7. **Appreciative of a challenge** – If you approach a
    difficult sales situation or a prestigious client with a
    defeated attitude, you will certainly limit your success
    and get passed over time and time again. Appreciate
    these challenges, roll up your sleeves and tackle them
    with gusto. Your sales figures will reflect your courage!

8. **Persistent -** Once you have met with your prospective
    clients, you need to be persistent and follow up by the
    end of the day. Thank them for their time and remind
    them of the positive elements you will bring to their
    event, and keep following up until you are told of their
    decision.

9. **Competitive** – In the special events industry you might
    find yourself regularly bidding against your friends, and
    you must get ready to unleash your fiery competitive
    spirit! Keep an eye on your colleagues, stay one step
    ahead of their innovations, and be prepared to undercut
    them (as long as it makes fiscal sense).

10. **Able to cope with rejection** - We have all been there: rejected. It feels terrible, but part of being a great salesperson is knowing how to get up, dust yourself off and keep your spirits high. After all, if you let this rejection affect your attitude you will lose more clients – and no one likes a vicious cycle like that!

11. **Great listening skills** – Have you ever sat and spoken to someone who clearly is not a good listener, a person who keeps interrupting you and putting words in your mouth? It's annoying and downright rude, and this person may have lost your business due to this behavior. Keep this in mind when you enter into a conversation with a prospective client – take notes, make eye contact and repeat their needs back to them to ensure you understand.

12. **Physically and mentally energetic** – Finally, in order to be a great salesperson you must have energy! Racing from meeting to meeting takes physical stamina, and remembering the countless small details involved in event planning is mentally tasking. Keep fit by exercising, meditating and taking care of yourself – without your health, your business is nothing!

Business can be likened to a game of bowling. You just can't play without knocking down the bowling pins. You need to set the pins again and replay when this happens. This is the same with being in the events industry. Flexibility, tenacity, perseverance are some of the characteristics of successful salespeople. When you face challenges, have the mind-set of surmounting them, because you can! You opted to pursue your dream because you believe in your abilities. When you keep in mind why you came into the events industry in the first place, you motivate yourself and your team and also equip yourself to make better decisions. Going back to the drawing board to re-examine the reasons you started your business is a way to build strength and forge ahead valiantly!

If you continue to do things the same way you always have, you will continue to get the results you have always had.

Meryl Snow

Testimonials:

"Wow!!! What a terrific presentation last evening. Your insights and suggestions for tomorrow's food marketing leaders were only matched by your passion and humor. Thank you.

> — Richard J. George, Chair & Professor of Food Marketing, Saint Joseph's University

—

"Meryl's unique gift is to communicate with each individual in the audience as if they were alone and talking one on one."

> — Patricia Littles- US Navy, Richmond, VA

—

"You have been the energy and passion that has been behind so much that has happened at Catersource. Working with you always energized me and also it was just plain fun because more than your incredible skills at what you do, I just plain really like you. "

> — Pauline Hoogmoed, CEO Catersource 2000-2014

—

"Thank you again for coming to Indy to join us and speak at our ISES Indiana Education Conference. We all really enjoyed having you here. I heard so many great comments. You really have a different approach to sales."

> — Jennifer McKinney-Seet-VP of Programs and Education for ISES

—

Meryl provided us with outstanding training; she was a pleasure to work with and to have had join our team for the day; I hope we can arrange future training."

> — United States Military Academy, West Point

"Outstanding! The conference attendees raved about your presentation. High scores all the way. I'll make sure I send Pauline an email and let her know. Thank you again. "

— NACUFS National Conference

After reviewing your video I was smiling ear to ear, fantastic presentation.

— Shannon Underwood, Speaker &
Topic Coordinator Wedding MBA

"As the largest catering and food service Management Company in Atlanta, we knew it would be a challenge to relate to our diversified business model; however, Meryl accepted the challenge and over delivered. From custom training program to meet our needs to day of training. Meryl truly went above and beyond. She motivated and inspired the team with a high level of confidence, industry knowledge and overall credibility. They each left with great takeaways that they have implemented in their respective locations. Her expertise is invaluable, with her broad array of experience, passion and instinctive grasp of this business."

— Dina Iglesias Director of Sales &
Marketing Proof of the Pudding Atlanta,
GA

"Thank you thank you thank you!!! Yesterday and today have been such an eye opening and positive experience for our team! the future is going to be amazing and Francesca and I are so motivated to take Lombardo's to the next level! Its only day one but they are engaged and motivated to use your teachings. "

— David Lombardo- Lombardo's
Catering Boston, MA

"You put together a powerful, and informative presentation. All the knowledge you have and share has made this a worthwhile return on this investment. I can feel the energy in the sales dept. and they are buzzing with each other. We are looking forward on acting on the information you have share with us. We are looking forward on acting on the information you have share with us.

I will stay in touch and let you know how we are doing."

— Susan Lawrence- Pepper's
Northboro, MA

"I just wanted to thank you again for coming to visit our Greater Triangle chapter. I have read over all of the surveys and everyone was thrilled with your presentation (as expected). Here are a few:

- The presentation was very helpful with stronger ways to not only sell yourself, but your business. I particularly liked the "Feature/Benefit" for I had not thought of presenting, or selling that way.
- It provided good information for me to pass along to my sales team. I enjoyed the speaker so much!
- Good focused edu about sales, and selling yourself, I enjoyed it and plan to put into practice."

— Valerie Curran- VP of Programs and
Education for ISES Greater Triangle
chapter

"Where do I begin? Thank you so much for speaking at our annual Education Conference yesterday. The attendees had great feedback on the content of your session and enjoyed listening and learning. We will keep you updated on when your sales techniques begin to be implemented as I know they will be."

— Lisa Brenner Education Chair NACE
Minneapolis Chapter

"Meryl, just wanted to dash off a quick note to thank you for coming to Miami and for your efforts and energy to assist us in; inspiring our team, motivating them to get out of their chairs and driving home the concept that selling directly effects their pocket as well as the company's. You did an awesome job and they are very pepped up. We changed the sales meeting format as you suggested. I absolutely appreciate that you think as an "owner". I always felt that your allegiance was with me and the company and that your efforts were for the betterment of the company by inspiring and educating my team. It worked and I will have you come back again."

— Joy Wallace, A Joy Wallace Catering & Production, Miami

—

"I'm struggling at the moment to find the words for this post...
For so many years now, I've gone to Vegas to the Catersource Conference and sat front row center of your classes. I've learned from you, been inspired by you and I've grown as a caterer and a professional. You make me want to be a better, more confident and more poised person in my everyday life. I am truly blessed to be able to call you my mentor, but also my friend! Meryl Snow, you are an absolute gem! I've dreamt about bringing you out for so long and the experience was much more than I could have imagined!! I CANNOT wait to see how our team grows after your visit!"

— Melissa Tibben - Attitude on Food - Omaha, NE

"People are still talking about how great you were, I started watching Tommy Boy last night on Netflix :)
You were fantastic, Meryl, thank you SO much!"

— Shaun Gray, President for ISES Houston Chapter

"Sitting in today's sales meeting reviewing all we learned from our visit with Meryl Snow. Wow- we are talking a lot. Thanks Meryl"

— Kelly Early Thomas Caterers of Distinction, Indianapolis, IN

"Our team took away so much from Meryl's "Sales is Sales" class. We debriefed afterward and compiled a page-long list of action items that we implemented immediately! It was also a great reminder of sales basics - making the time to form relationships, how to address hard questions - that give us confidence and strength as a sales team. I know we'll see growth in confirmed events and overall sales because of what we learned at Meryl's class. "

Colbert Callen Director of Events Footers, Denver, CO

"Oh my gosh Meryl, things are good and crazy around here. We have been busy moving people around, creating new job descriptions, assigning venues, and on and on."

Dawn Tangeman The Wild Thyme Company, San Diego, CA

"We've had several consultants help us throughout the years, but Meryl Snow's training was by far the most beneficial to our sales team. Her fresh ideas and suggestions energized our sales efforts and business has already increased. I highly recommend Meryl—she will change your company for the better."

Shellie Morrison, President The Event Group—Division, Inc., Arkansas

I would love to hear when these techniques work for you.

Email me! Meryl@MerylSnow.com

Made in the USA
Middletown, DE
16 April 2019